Once I W[o]...
Baby

Written by Valerie Fawcett

Harcourt
Supplemental Publishers

Rigby • Steck-Vaughn

www.steck-vaughn.com

Once I was a baby.
What did I do?

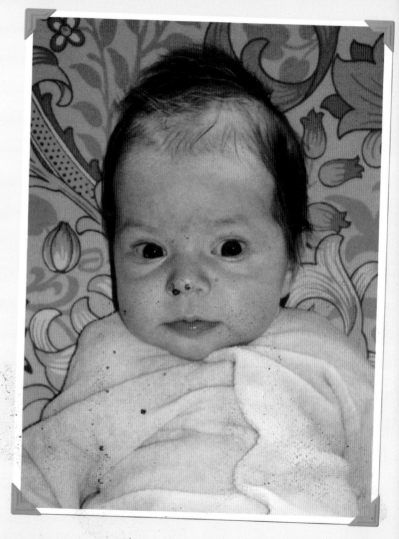

I looked up at my mom's face.
I looked up at my toy.

3

Once I was one.
What did I do?

4

I looked at some flowers.
I played in the garden.

Once I was two.
What did I do?

I made a snowman.
I played with some toys.

Once I was four.
What did I do?

8

I made a tower.

I grew a flower in the garden.

Now I am six.
What do I do?

I make pictures.

I make some faces and flowers.

baby

one

two

six

four

12